THE DANGEROUS GAP BETWEEN AMERICAN SOCIETY AND ITS MILITARY

> These are the times that try men's souls. The summer soldier and the sunshine patriot will, in the crisis, shrink from the service of his country; but he that stands it now, deserves the love and thanks of man and woman.

—Thomas Paine[1]

The United States has been at war for over ten years since that fateful day of September 11, 2001. Despite the surge in American patriotism and resultant overwhelming admiration for the military during these ten years, a dangerous gap between American society and its military has grown. In the history of the United States no major war has ever been fought with a smaller percentage of its citizens. With a military force of approximately 2.4 million members out of a national population of 300 million, less than one percent of Americans have served during Operation Enduring Freedom (OEF) and Operation Iraqi Freedom (OIF).[2] During Representative Ike Skelton's farewell speech, the outgoing chairman of the House Armed Services Committee warned of what he saw as "A civilian-military gap, a lack of understanding between civilians and the military that has grown wider in the era of an all-volunteer force." Has the civilian-military gap developed to the point in America that we now have two distinct classes of citizens: those who protect the nation and those who live under that protection? If so, how much does the all-volunteer force play in this problem and are we allowing it to grow to the point that it will adversely impact American national security and weaken our democracy.[3]

The All-Volunteer Force

Service in defense of one's nation was universally accepted in America from before the Revolution until the early 1960s. The move to an all-volunteer force was the result of five factors: 1) Demographics, 2) Costs, 3) Morale and economic rationale, 4) Opposition to the Vietnam War, and 5) The military's desire for a more professional force.[4] By the 1960s the demographics in America had changed resulting in a larger population of draft eligible young men than the military needed. Meanwhile, the military services had no problems in meeting their enlistment requirements through volunteers. From both a morale and economic standpoint, Conservatives and Libertarians argued that the nation had no right to impose military service on its young men without their consent. Liberals asserted that the draft placed unfair burdens on the underprivileged members of American society who were unable to work the draft's bureaucratic system in order to gain a deferment.[5] As American military involvement in Vietnam grew, opposition to the war coincided with political demands to eliminate the draft.

Initially, the strongest opponent to an all-volunteer force, the military had lost confidence in the draft and would not put up a fight to eliminate the draft and move to an all-volunteer force. Discipline problems with draftees increased as the war in Vietnam went on; raising concerns regarding the quality of recruit the military received via the draft.

Prior to the decision to eliminate the draft and adapt an all-volunteer force, members of Congress and Veteran's groups raised concerns, that this would create a cultural gap between service members and the nation's civilian population. Elimination of the draft and implementation of an all-volunteer force would, they argued, usher in a professional military force that would be unrepresentative of American society.[6] An all-volunteer force would surely undermine national unity by eliminating the one thing that most American men shared with one another, military service. Some politicians argued that the burden of combat in a volunteer force would fall upon the poor and minorities while others believed that those with better education and backgrounds would never volunteer to serve in the military. Despite pressure to keep the draft in place in a time of war, a newly elected President would keep his promise to change America's military to an all-volunteer force.[7]

President Nixon had made a campaign pledge during the 1968 election to end the draft. Shortly after entering office, on March 27, 1969, he announced the Gates Commission. Led by former Secretary of Defense Thomas Gates, Jr., it was charged with developing a comprehensive plan for eliminating conscription and moving toward an all-volunteer armed force.[8] By December 1969, the commission completed its review and presented a unanimous recommendation that the nation's interests would be better served by an all-volunteer force. The commission stated, "The United States has relied throughout its history on a voluntary armed force except during major wars and since 1948. A return to an all-volunteer force will strengthen our freedoms. It is the system for maintaining standing forces that minimizes government interference with the freedom of the individual to determine his own life in accord with his values."[9] The Gates Commission recommendation would lead President Nixon to eliminating the draft in 1973. The full effect of this act would not become apparent until a generation later during Operation Desert Storm. The success of changing to an all-volunteer force became evident during Operation Desert Storm when a professional force along with a coalition defeated and evicted a battle hardened Iraqi army from Kuwait in only four days.[10]

The success of the change to an all-volunteer force did not stop with the battlefield triumphs in the Middle East in 2001. The quality of the men and women who volunteered to serve only continued to improve. Since 1978 the Department of Defense has recorded and published an annual report on America's social representation in the military. Predictably, it reported that the active duty military population is younger than the overall civilian sector with 49% of the active duty force between the ages of 17 and 24. Only 15% of the American civilian workforce falls between those ages. An all-volunteer force has proven itself to be a higher-aptitude and more-educated force. The all-volunteer force today has nearly half of its recruits in the top two Armed Forces Qualification Test (AFQT) categories, only 1% scored in the lowest AFQT category while 96% of the enlisted force, are high school graduates. Only 33% of enlisted members who were accessed in the final two years of the draft scored in the top categories with nearly 25% scoring in the lowest category. Only half of those who were drafted in the final two years had high school diplomas.[11]

By nearly every measure, the all-volunteer force has been an overwhelming success for the military. Since the establishment of the all-volunteer force, the quality of America's service members has dramatically improved. The percentage of new recruits with high school diplomas increased, as did the IQ scores from the days of the draft. The all-volunteer force increased the number of career personnel and increased the proficiency and professionalism of the force.

When it comes to education, the 2004 report showed that 92% of enlistees are high school graduates, a dramatic increase from the 1973 goal of 45% and the 2004 goal of 79%. In terms of aptitude, results from a defense research project, validated by the National Academy of Sciences, reported that scores on the AFQT are strong predictors of training success and on-the-job performance. Today's Armed Forces are successful and perform at a high level because they are comprised of high-aptitude individuals.[12] When this is combined with experience there is no more lethal and effective military than America's armed forces.

A key factor in the success of the all-volunteer force is retention and the experience that retention brings. Under conscription, retention was a challenge greatly impacting the ability to grow the necessary experience within both the officer and enlisted corps. The majority of individuals who were drafted only served for a short period of time as compared to today's force. Today's mid-grade and senior noncommissioned officers posses more experience than their draft era counterparts. Shorter enlistments result in high personnel turnover that negatively affects a unit's readiness. According to one study, in 1969 less than 20% of enlisted Army soldiers had more than four years of experience while today it is just over 50%. When the subject of re-instituting the draft was raised to Secretary Gates, he responded, "Going back to compulsory service, in addition to being politically impossible, is highly impractical given the kinds of technical skills, experience, and attributes needed to be successful on the battlefield in the 21st century. For that reason, re-instituting the draft is overwhelmingly opposed by the military's leadership."[13]

The all-volunteer force has also served as a laboratory for social change in America. Issues have ranged from integrating African-Americans and women to the most recent issue of allowing homosexuals to serve openly; the military has routinely been the environment for these experiments.[14] The military has often adopted these changes earlier than other institutions making it an avenue of upward mobility for many. When Admiral Mullen spoke at West Point's graduation ceremony in 2011, in the class, 310 of the 1,031 graduating cadets were minorities, including 225 women.[15]

In broad demographic terms, members of the Armed Forces have been largely representative of the country as a whole economically, drawing primarily from the working and middle classes. There do continue to be disparities when it comes to race in certain specialties and in some of the higher ranks. The concerns raised in the 1960s as the concept of an all-volunteer force was being considered have not materialized. The members who serve in the military have not predominately come from America's poorest and worst educated nor have they those who have been unable to find employment. In today's difficult economic times with near 9% unemployment, the military continues to meet both its quantitative and qualitative recruiting goals despite having been engaged in two wars.

The all-volunteer force has also changed the composition and culture of the military in other ways. Military members are more likely to be married than are their civilian counterparts. Today's all-volunteer force is largely a married force in comparison to the force in 1973. While marriage rates are declining in America a majority of enlisted personnel are married up to 53.1% from 40.1% in 1973.[16] While a force of predominately married service members has its benefits, it also comes with the costs of funding for family programs, family housing and medical care which are all contribute to the rising personnel costs.

The Gap

The growing civilian-military gap is one of the most serious and consequential issues facing America today. The further removed from the military the American population becomes, the less they will empathize with the sacrifices service members make and the less concern they will show for national security issues. In the absence of a draft, to most Americans military service has become something for other people to do. As a result many Americans are not only unaware of the decisions being made regarding the use of the military and its impact on American foreign policy. While some may question the Defense Department's budget few question how the military is being used and the possible consequences those decisions may have.

Following the American Revolution through the end of World War II, the United States maintained a small standing army that would use mass conscription to expand during times of war. After World War II, and with the start of the Cold War, America maintained a large standing military through a draft even though it was peacetime.[17] Throughout the Cold War, the call to serve America extended to every class of society. From farmers and ranchers, lawyers and constructions workers to professional athletes, celebrities, future politicians and businessmen, able bodied men from all walks of life served their country. Many actually volunteered in order to join the service of their choice vice waiting to be drafted and assigned to a service.[18] The opportunity and obligation to serve was expected and accepted.

Today, the military is one of the most respected institutions in America.[19] Since 1998, Gallup surveys have ranked the military as the nation's most trusted institution. Another poll completed by the National Opinion Research Center at the University of Chicago, reported 75% of respondents were "very proud" of America's armed forces; giving them the highest mark in their poll.[20] Despite the praise and admiration, the surge in those signing up to serve in the years following September 11, 2001 has dwindled.

During former Secretary of Defense Robert Gates' September 2010 speech at Duke University, he voiced his concern that America must address the state of its all-volunteer force and the consequences that go with having so few Americans fighting her wars for so long. The challenge the gap presents must be acknowledged and dealt with, if the United States is going to sustain the kind of military America needs in what will surely be an even more dangerous 21st century.[21]

Many prominent and well-positioned observers believe that the gap has grown wider since the beginning of the war on terror. During his Duke University speech, then Secretary of Defense Gates raised his concerns regarding the growing disconnect between today's professional soldiers and the civilian society they serve. Secretary Gates stated, "Even after 9/11, in the absence of a draft, for a growing number of Americans, service in the military, no matter how laudable, has become something for other people to do."[22] The former Chairman of the Joint Chiefs of Staff, Admiral Mullen raised this same concern during his address to the graduating class of West Point in 2011, stating in reference to the civilian-military gap, "I fear they do not know us." Admiral Mullen said of our nation's civilians, "I fear they do not comprehend the full weight of the burden we carry or the price we pay when we return from battle."[23]

A Cohen Research Group survey from 2010 confirmed the fears that both Secretary Gates and Chairman Mullen had raised. After nine years of war, 36% of Americans do not know someone personally who had served in either Afghanistan or Iraq. This is vastly different than previous wars when entire American communities shared the weight of the defense of their nation.[24] For those who volunteered to serve, the burden of numerous deployments, time away from family and friends and the likelihood of facing combat is accepted. Few could imagine that they would be fighting the first large-scale war since the American Revolution that relied solely on volunteers.[25]

How Americans and the Military See Each Other

Another effect of the growing gap is a change in how civilians and military personnel see the wars and each other. A Pew survey would report that 90% of civilians' surveyed expressed "pride in the military," another 75% stated they have "thanked someone in the military," yet only 25% acknowledged following the news of the wars closely. Only 50% of those surveyed acknowledged that the wars had made a difference in their lives.[26] Fortunately for most Americans, the wars of the past ten years have only been news stories and not something that has affected them or their families personally.

While most American's have lost touch with what their military is going through, the same can be said about American service members and the people they have sworn to defend. In a 2011 Pew survey, 84% of post-9/11 veterans believe the American public does not understand the problems faced by those who serve and their family members. On the same question 71% of the public surveyed agreed with the military's assessment. On another question, 83% would agree that military personnel and their families made sacrifices since September 11, 2001 however, only 26% surveyed responded that the military was unfairly taking on the burden of the war. Surprisingly, 70% of those surveyed consider that burden as "just part of being in the military," reconfirming the belief that most Americans have little understanding of the toll the war is taking on our service members."[27]

Many Americans believe service members and their families are different than mainstream America. Many assume military members and their families are socially conservative. Our own Congress declared in the fiscal year 2004 National Defense Authorization Act that, "Military life is fundamentally different from civilian life," and "the military society is characterized by its own laws, rules, customs, and traditions, including numerous restrictions on personal behavior that would not be acceptable in civilian society."[28] David Wood, an embedded reporter with the Huffington Post, who deployed with the military throughout the last few years, reported that America's military is engaged in two wars far from America. One is against the enemy, the other, is against a professional ethos that is becoming ingrained in the military's officer corps. Mr. Wood would go on to warn that this strengthened commitment to military virtue in conjunction with the cultural isolation of the military is creating what he termed a "warrior class." Soldiers, Sailors, Airmen and Marines are military professionals, who see themselves as different and incompatible with the remainder of society. A soldier's daily life depends on self-discipline and sacrifice and they disdain what they perceive as the loose values, sloppy discipline and quick-buck self-centeredness of the society back home.[29]

The Family Business

Since the elimination of the draft and the implementation of the all-volunteer force fewer Americans are directly related to someone with military experience. In 1988 nearly 40% of 18 year olds in America had a parent who had served in the military. That number has dropped to 18% only twelve years.[30] As these numbers continue to drop, the number of military members who have family that have served is growing. The combination of these two trends indicates that increasingly, military service is becoming a family tradition. Further support of this was made evident in a survey of more than 2,000 civilian adults and almost 1,900 veterans that included more than 700 participants who had served after September 11, 2001. Most respondents identified having family members who were serving in the military or have served in the past. Traditionally older Americans were more likely to have close military ties as more than 75% of civilian adults ages 50 and older reported having an immediate family member who had served or is currently serving in the military. For most, that service took place prior to the 1973 decision to eliminate the draft and implementation of the all-volunteer force. Fifty-seven percent of civilian respondents between the ages 30 and 49 reported having an immediate family member who had served in the military and only 33% of those between the ages of 18 to 29 reported having an immediate family who has served.

Seventy-nine percent of veterans surveyed reported that an immediate family member is serving or has served in the military compared to only 61% of civilian respondents.[31] For many, to include minorities, military service is a family tradition. Among currently serving service members, 68% of whites, 59% of blacks and 30% of Hispanic respondents reported having immediate family members who serve or have served in uniform.[32]

What Will it Take to Close the Gap and at What Cost?

Heavy reliance upon technology and rising personnel costs has created an economic challenge for the nation. At what cost can America continue to maintain an all-volunteer force. Many of the factors that made an all-volunteer force successful have, in fact, become huge cost drivers. Increased pay and entitlements, health care, enlistment and retention bonuses, increased scholarships, in-service and post-service

11

educational benefits, family housing and increased morale, welfare and recreation programs all come at significant and rising costs. Between 2001 and 2011 the Army's personnel costs more than doubled, from $27.7 billion to $59.1 billion. Shortly after the start of OEF in 2002 through 2011 housing allowances increased by 83% along with a 40% increase in the military's Basic Allowance for Subsistence.[33] Today nearly forty cents of every dollar spent in the Defense Department goes towards personnel.

The use of an all-volunteer force has allowed large segments of America's population to avoid the moral obligation to serve in defense their own country. As fewer Americans can relate to their own military many have little interest in the decisions that are made regarding the use of the military. Coupled with the fact that fewer Americans have served in the military, the same can be said of the people who have been elected to represent the American people. In the past, Veterans were once over-represented in Congress as they were following World War II and Vietnam but today they are now under-represented by our elected government. Only 22% of members of Congress today have served in the military, the lowest number since World War II.[34]

Some have suggested that in order to ensure all Americans share the burden of war that the draft be re-instituted. In 2003, prior to the start of OIF, Representative Charles Rangel raised concerns regarding the continued use of an all-volunteer force, "We must be certain that the sacrifices we will be asking our armed forces to make are shared by the rest of us."[35] If this were the case, that this responsibility was shared, then it would also ensure that those individuals elected to represent the people would have a greater understanding and appreciate for the consequences when sending America's men and women off to war.

One solution that has been raised would be for Congress to bring back the draft. The belief is that this is the only way to ensure that every member of every Congressional district will be impacted by the decision to send men and women off to war and only through that direct involvement will those in Congress consider the decisions being made. For those who advocate the return to a draft, they fail to acknowledge that compulsory service did not produce an equal sharing of sacrifice. One only has to look at the number of individuals who were able to avoid service in Vietnam through a long list of exemptions. In addition, as Secretary Gates has stated, "going back to compulsory service, in addition to being politically impossible, is highly impractical given the kinds of technical skills, experience, and attributes needed to be successful on the battlefield in the 21st century and it is overwhelmingly opposed by the military's leadership."[36] The solution is not to re-impose the draft but to ensure that the decisions to use the armed forces are those are made in the best interests of the entire nation and that the burden be shared by the entire nation in both blood and treasure.

How We Made the Gap Worse

Military service for many Americans provided an economic and educational springboard. Unfortunately, these opportunities have decreased and are likely to get smaller. Following the conclusion of any major conflict the United States government has routinely downsized the military reducing the size of the standing force. After the fall of the Berlin Wall in 1989 and the end of the Cold War, the American military was reduced from 2.1 million to 1.4 million personnel leading to dramatic reduction in accessions of both officers and enlisted members. As operations in Iraq have ended and with the projected withdrawal from Afghanistan in 2014, the Federal Government has already tasked the Department of Defense to begin a drawdown in force structure along with a cut to the overall Defense Department budget. One projection has the Army downsizing from 520,000 active duty members down to 490,000 by 2016. Cuts to the Defense Department are projected between $487 billion and $1 trillion over the next decade.[37]

As a result of these projected cuts, changes are being planned that will contribute to the divide between our nation's military and civilian society. Fiscal constraints are affecting recruiting budgets, further reducing the military's exposure to the public. Advertising campaigns such as those involved in the NASCAR racing circuit have come under scrutiny by Congressional leaders and targeted for reduction. Television commercials during peak audience time slots and during professional sporting events have been drastically reduced due to advertising budgets being slashed across all services.[38]

Budgetary cuts in outreach programs have not been limited to traditional advertising media. These cuts also impact the recruiting of officers. Storefront recruiting offices are being closed, as are Reserve Officer Training Corps (ROTC) detachments across the country. Today fewer ROTC detachments exist in America's major cities. Between Los Angeles and Chicago there are over 21 million people yet these two major cities host only 7 ROTC detachments. The state of Alabama, with a population of less than 5 million people, has 10 Army ROTC host programs. Budget cuts re forcing the military to recruit with fewer stations and in less costly areas. Recruiting decisions have reinforced this growing concentration among certain regions and even with families. Recruiters now armed with limited resources must focus their efforts where they are most likely to have success; with those potential recruits who can relate to the military. The most likely recruits tend to have friends, classmates, and parents who have served. This practice directly contributes to the theory that military service is becoming a family tradition among a small portion of American society.[39]

After the repeal of "Don't Ask, Don't Tell" (DADT) in 2011, many anticipated a reopening of ROTC detachments at Ivy League schools. For some, the hope was that the presence of an ROTC detachment at these prestigious schools would make military service more inviting to America's gifted college students. Despite the repeal of the DADT law and the lobbying of the President himself, ROTC detachments have not sprung up across Ivy League campuses. Some schools are still re-considering their position on military recruiting and officer training on their campuses. Even if these institutions implement major reversals and allow a return of ROTC to their campuses, it remains to be seen if their students will step forward and volunteer to serve.[40] Without representation from both our small towns and our biggest cities and every class of American society, how can we expect to develop military leaders who come from across the landscape of America and how can they relate to the people they are sworn to defend.

Other effects to conserve tax dollars by the Federal Government have contributed to the growing gap. Decisions made by the Base Realignment and Closure (BRAC) Committee regarding base closures and base consolidations resulted in closure of ninety-seven bases and greatly reduced the military's access and exposure to a large portion of the American population.[41] Closure of some military installations resulted in the military moving away from urban locations and further isolating the military from population-dense areas. As a result of budget cuts and BRAC decisions, in addition to global basing changes, a significant percentage of the Army stationed in the United States have been moved to installations in just five states: Texas, Washington, Georgia, Kentucky, and North Carolina.[42] In some cases, moves were made in support of environmental and budgetary concerns but together these moves have resulted in closure of numerous military installations near some of America's largest population centers.

The impact of BRAC mandates is significant. Sixty-four percent of Southerners reported immediate family ties to the military while those living in the Northeast were 56% and in the West 57%. Those who live in cities of over one million are less likely than those in the suburbs or rural areas to say a family member served in the military.[43] BRAC has greatly contributed to the growing civilian-military gap and has greatly diminished the relationship and familiarity many communities had with their military.

What Happened to the War Powers Act?

As the majority of Americans have grown distant from their military, they have also become immune to the decisions made regarding the use of their military. This lack of interest has enabled political leaders to employ America's military without much fear of backlash from their constituents despite their constitutional responsibilities. Congress had specifically passed the War Powers Act to establish a set of procedures, consistent with the Constitution, for both the President and Congress to follow in situations where the deployment of American armed forces could lead to their involvement in combat. The American Congress imposed this resolution to "insure that the collective judgment of both the Congress and the President will apply to the introduction of United States Armed Forces into hostilities."[44]

In accordance with the Constitution of the United States, the war powers of the federal government are divided between the Executive and Legislative branches. Under Article II, Section 2, the President is the Commander in Chief of the armed forces and the President's powers as Commander in Chief are exercised only pursuant to a declaration of war, specific statutory authorization from Congress, or a national emergency created by an attack upon the United States.[45] Congress has the power to make declarations of war, and the responsibility to raise and support the armed forces per Article I, section 8.[46] Section 3 specifically requires that the President, "in every possible instance shall consult with Congress before introducing United States Armed Forces into hostilities or into situation where imminent involvement in hostilities is clearly indicated by the circumstances, and after every such introduction shall consult regularly with the Congress until United States Armed Forces are no longer engaged in hostilities or have been removed from such situations."[47] Despite this requirement, the President has and continues to deploy armed forces into hostile situations without a formal declaration of war or other form of Congressional approval. Congress has failed to enact its powers of the purse to limit the President's ability to send American men and women into harms way.

Congress has not declared an official war since the 1940s, yet the President has regularly deployed the military into hostile areas without Congressional approval. In 2011, questions were again raised regarding President Obama's decisions to deploy American forces into harms way in Africa. Following a United Nations Security Council

Resolution 1973 (2011), which publicly deplored the failure of the Libyan authorities to comply with resolution 1970 (2011), President Obama committed American service men and women to the Libyan operation without consulting Congress. Despite the UN resolution for support in Libya, its own charter calls for those nations who participate in security operations to follow their own legislative process before committing forces. Article forty-three, chapter seven of the United Nations Charter, specifically states that, "The agreement or agreements shall be negotiated as soon as possible on the initiative of the Security Council. They shall be concluded between the Security Council and Members or between the Security Council and groups of Members and shall be subject to ratification by the signatory states in accordance with their respective constitutional processes."[48]

As fewer Americans are aware of, let alone personally impacted by, combat operations in the Middle East or North Africa, fewer were concerned with holding their elected officials accountable for those decisions affecting their military. This has been an evolutionary process that began over two hundred years ago when President Thomas Jefferson declared war on the Barbary States in 1801. President Jefferson informed Congress of his actions and secured Congressional authorization for the use of force against the Barbary pirates. Over time, American Presidents would send the military out for various types of missions and military operations other than war without Congressional approval. The civilian-military gap only serves to exacerbate the traditional friction between the Legislative and Executive Branches. Americans view their legislative representatives as their connection with their government and the process of implementing American laws and policies. When both the President and

Congress make decisions and take actions despite the wishes of the citizens they violate the trust that their constituents have placed in them.

Can We Close the Gap?

Politicians on both sides of the political aisle demand a military force that can contain the emerging threats; transform failed states; chase terrorists; train foreign militaries to assist in the war against violent extremists, ensure the freedom of navigation of the ocean, protect American interests in foreign oil, conduct humanitarian missions; respond to natural disasters at home and abroad and the list goes on and on. The only way for the military to be able to address any number of these issues simultaneously, as demanded, is for it to be with a budget that will support the technology and manpower needed to carry out these tasks. Without the resources to ensure the men and women who are tasked with these missions are properly trained, equipped and cared for, these tasks will not be met.[49] While the military will drawdown and resources will be limited, there are other opportunities that may allow American citizens to become involved with their military, their government and their communities.

When President Obama entered office, he stated that he was committed to expanding national and community service opportunities. He believed that as our nation continues on the road to economic recovery, volunteer service would play a vital role in addressing both national and local challenges. In June 2009, the President launched "United We Serve" as a nationwide initiative to create a sustained and focused effort to meet community needs and make service a way of life for all Americans.[50] The concept of national service as a solution to some of our nation's problems doesn't reside solely with the Democrats as the leading 2012 Republican Presidential candidates, Rick

Santorum and Mitt Romney, have both expressed support for national service programs. President George W. Bush called on citizens to help others after the terrorist attacks of September 11, 2001 and Hurricane Katrina in August 2005.[51]

A possible solution towards solving the civilian-military gap is national service, or what Professor Richard Dagger from Arizona State University's Political Science Depart identified as "Civic Service." Civic service would not be limited to military service and would allow for the opportunity to serve in one's own community at the local and state levels instead of being limited to only national service. In Professor Dagger's paper "Republican Virtue, Liberal Freedom, and the Problem of Civic Service," he outlines why the term "civic" should be used instead of "national" as to use "civic" is to stress the connection to the ideals of citizenship and one's civic duty and civic virtue.[52] Professor Dagger further explains his theory that, "to do one's duty as a citizen, not as a member of a particular nation or people. The two ideas, citizenship and nationality, are not exclusive of each other, to be sure, and identification with a nation may well inspire people to act as citizens."[53]

Compulsory service, or a return of the draft, would fall short of closing the gap as well as greatly reducing both the quality and capability of the force. Civic service on the other hand would include the opportunity to serve in the military along with opportunities to serve in a variety of professions such as in education, law enforcement, fire and rescue, hospital orderly, conservation efforts and public works to name a few. Professor Dagger presents a compelling argument for civic service that would allow American's to do their duty by doing something for other members of their community in return for the protection of the law and the freedoms that Americans enjoy everyday of their lives.

Civic service would be voluntary and open to all who are physically and mentally capable of service. Successful completion of this civic service would allow that individual the right to vote in elections, to hold public office or to serve in any civil service position. Those who choose not to serve would not be denied their civil rights but they would not be allowed to participate in elections, serve in an elected position or fill a civil service position.[54] This would ensure that those individuals who have the responsibility of creating and changing the laws of the land as well as the authority to send America's sons and daughters off to war will have served their nation and posses a greater appreciation for the consequences of their decisions.

Another Solution: Regaining America's Militia Tradition

One solution that has been proposed is to downsize the active duty military to a smaller emergency force and rely more heavily upon the National Guard and Reserves. The task of maintaining a right sized and resourced military will continue to challenge the United States as it faces continued economic constraints. A smaller, ready military is preferable to a large force that lacks the necessary resources to ensure it is trained and equipped to meet the challenges it faces today and in the future.[55] Interestingly, this requirement for a trained and ready military may not conflict with the desire to reconnect with the American people. This proposal could have a positive effect towards addressing the civilian-military gap as it would increased the exposure of the military and military service in America's hometowns.

The majority of those who serve in the Guard and Reserves continue to volunteer to serve their nation while maintaining another full-time profession. Most Guard and Reserve members are established in their communities and in some cases far from any active military installation. Most work in professions not associated with the military. These are members of society who are established and in many cases active participants in their communities. By virtue of the service and experience they can serve as advertisement for benefits and options that military service may provide. Whenever one of these members were to leave work and their communities for their annual tours or deployments, the impact of their absence would be felt and shared by those around them.

The challenge that greater reliance upon our citizen soldiers' presents is the impact their service may have on the home front. If these members are committed to national defense issues, what capabilities does this take away from State Governors that rely heavily upon the Guard for a variety of state emergencies? With greater reliance upon the Guard and Reserves to meet national defense would drive a greater training requirement. This would require a larger budget in order to not only pay to activate these members for deployments but also to cover the increased training requirements. An increased demand on the Guard and Reserve will have an impact on their communities. Longer absences due to increased training and longer deployments will impact the businesses and organizations that rely upon their employees and staff to be present. While a move to greater reliance upon America's citizen soldiers could help with the gap it would not solve the challenge that today's economic constraints present.

The challenge is finding a solution to the gap while ensuring the quality of force America has come to know and trust is not diminished. In order for any solution to successful it must begin with the direct involvement of the American people. Today, only 1% of Americans volunteer to serve, finding the men and women necessary to fight tomorrow's wars in a downsized military will be harder to find. A downward trend in high-quality enlistment supply already exists due to a rise in college attendance amongst the 18-24 year-old American populations. There is also a growing number of youth who fail to meet the minimum military entrance standards. America is already suffering from an ever-growing number of 17 to 24 year olds, approximately 75% of the that population who are simply ineligible or unavailable to serve for a variety of reasons such as education, criminal records but above all health and weight problems in an age of spiraling childhood obesity.[56]

Conclusion

The gap between American society and its military has continued to grow despite the events of September 11, 2001 and ten plus years of war. The gap has created as Representative Skelton accurately described as a society of two distinct classes of citizens: those who serve and those who do not?[57] Today fewer Americans can relate to their military and many are unaware of the decisions being used regarding the military. While many question the Department of Defense's overall budget when compared to Education and Social Welfare programs, few understand how and if the military is truly being used in the best interests of the nation.

Congress and the Department of Defense must determine the appropriate size and composition of the American military in order to ensure it is capable of a range of missions in order to ensure it is fully prepared to deter and defeat aggression. It must also be capable of continuing modernization efforts in order to address emerging threats that America's enemies present. The challenge will not only be in ensuring that the budget is available to meet threats in the future but will America be able to field a voluntary force of the caliber to meet those threats. The value and importance of the all-volunteer force cannot be emphasized enough. General Martin Dempsey, Chairman of the Joint Chiefs of Staff emphasizes its importance when stating, "The all-volunteer Joint Force is our Nation's decisive advantage. Those who serve in the Armed Forces of the United States of America are the source of our unrivaled strength. The talented men and women of the Joint Force are resilient warriors who volunteer to fight and fight again."[58]

Americans must hold their representatives accountable for the decisions made regarding the use of the military. Congress has a responsibility in accordance with the War Powers Resolution Act to reign-in the president's disregard for its constitutional power to declare war. In accordance with Article I, Section 8 of the War Powers Resolution Act, Congress is responsible for the funding of the military and the conflicts it may be engaged in. Closing the civilian-military gap by more active participation in national defense would encourage the people and their representatives to not allow the President to circumvent Congress and place America's men and women in harms way without observing Constitutional checks and balances. Nor should the President be given a pass when those decisions are being justified under the auspices of the United Nations or even NATO.

Congress is in a tough position when challenging the President when the military has been sent into harms way. While it would be political suicide to cut off funds immediately and put the lives of Americans in danger but it can pass a bill denying future funding after three months, all in accordance with the War Powers Resolution Act. The willingness to do this may prevent the President from unnecessarily expanding the mission and needlessly placing American service members in harms way. Failure to

do so will only add to what has becoming a serious problem. As Americans have failed

to relate to their military and understand how they are being used, they have allowed

the conditions to set in that will threaten American national security and its democracy.

Endnotes

[1]Thomas Paine, "The Crisis" 4 December 1776, Library Of Congress http://www.loc.gov/teachers/classroommaterials/presentationsandactivities/presentations/timeline/amrev/north/paine.html (Accessed November 2, 2011)

[2] Lecture at Duke University (All-volunteer Force) As Delivered by Secretary of Defense Robert M. Gates, Durham, North Carolina, Wednesday, September 29, 2010 http://www.defense.gov/speeches/speech.aspx?speechid=1508 (Accessed November 2, 2011)

[3] Charlie Lewis, "A New Sparta: America's Threatening Civilian-military Gap," *Harvard, Kennedy School Review 2011 Edition*, http://isites.harvard.edu/icb/icb.do?keyword=k74756&pageid=icb.page414666 (Accessed November 25, 2011)

[4] Bernard Rostker, "The Evolution of the All-Volunteer Force" *2006, Rand Reports* http://www.rand.org/pubs/research_briefs/RB9195/index1.html (Accessed December 27, 2011)

[5] The President's Commission on an All-Volunteer Force, February 1970, http://www.rand.org/ pubs/ monographs/MG265/images/webS0243.pdf (Accessed December 27, 2011)

[6] Thomas Evans, "The All-Volunteer Army After Twenty Years: Recruiting in the Modern Era," [Excerpted from *Army History: The Professional Bulletin of Army History*, No. 27 (Summer 1993), pp. 40-46] http://www.shsu.edu/~his_ncp/VolArm.html (Accessed February 28, 2012)

[7] The President's Commission on an All-Volunteer Force, February 1970, http://www.rand.org/ pubs/ monographs/MG265/images/webS0243.pdf (Accessed December 27, 2011)

[8] Bernard Rostker, "I Want You, The Evolution of the All-volunteer Force" 2006, *Rand Reports*, http://www.rand.org/pubs/research_briefs/RB9195/index1.html (Accessed December 27, 2011)

[9] The President's Commission on an All-Volunteer Force, February 1970, http://www.rand.org/ pubs/ monographs/MG265/images/webS0243.pdf (Accessed December 27, 2011)

[10] Leo J. Daugherty III, "All Volunteer Force Success Story at 35," *Soldier's Magazine*, June 26, 2008 http://www.army.mil/article/10385/All_volunteer_force__success_story_at_35/ (Accessed February 29, 2012)

[11] Curtis L. Gilroy, "Defending the All Volunteer Force", *Armed Forces Journal*, March 2010, http://www.armedforcesjournal.com/2010/04/4537015 (Accessed January 21, 2012)

[12] Ibid.

[13] Lecture at Duke University (All Volunteer Force) As Delivered by Secretary of Defense Robert M. Gates, http://www.defense.gov/speeches/speech.aspx?speechid=1508 (Accessed November 2, 2011)

[14] Curtis L. Gilroy, "Defending the All Volunteer force", *Armed Forces Journal*, March 2010, http://www.armedforcesjournal.com/2010/04/4537015 (Accessed January 21, 2012)

[15] Karlyn Bowman and Andrew Rugg, "A U.S. military worth saluting: The U.S. military is the most respected institution in American life, according to several polls." *Los Angeles Times* May 30, 2011 http://articles.latimes.com/2011/may/30/opinion/la-oe-bowman-military-20110530 (Accessed November 2, 2011)

[16] Pew Research Center, "War and Sacrifice in the Post-9/11 Era The Military-Civilian Gap" October 5, 2011 http://www.pewsocialtrends.org/2011/10/05/war-and-sacrifice-in-the-post-911-era/ (Accessed November 2, 2011)

[17] Lecture at Duke University (All Volunteer Force) As Delivered by Secretary of Defense Robert M. Gates, http://www.defense.gov/speeches/speech.aspx?speechid=1508 (Accessed November 2, 2011)

[18] Ibid.

[19] Jeffrey M. Jones, "Americans Most Confident in Military, Least in Congress" Gallup.com, June 23, 2011, http://www.gallup.com/poll/148163/Americans-Confident-Military-Least-Congress.aspx?ref=more (accessed January 20, 2012)

[20] Karlyn Bowman and Andrew Rugg, "A U.S. military worth saluting: The U.S. military is the most respected institution in American life, according to several polls." *Los Angeles Times* May 30, 2011 http://articles.latimes.com/2011/may/30/opinion/la-oe-bowman-military-20110530 (Accessed November 2, 2011)

[21] Lecture at Duke University (All Volunteer Force) As Delivered by Secretary of Defense Robert M. Gates, http://www.defense.gov/speeches/speech.aspx?speechid=1508 (Accessed November 2, 2011)

[22] Ibid.

[23] Pew Research Center, "War and Sacrifice in the Post-9/11 Era The Military-Civilian Gap" October 5, 2011 http://www.pewsocialtrends.org/2011/10/05/war-and-sacrifice-in-the-post-911-era/ (Accessed November 2, 2011)

[24] Public Awareness Poll: Needs and Support for our OIF/OEF Military and Veteran Community Cohen Research http://www.cohenresearchgroup.com/media/ciav_201006.pdf (Accessed December 27, 2011)

[25] Lecture at Duke University (All Volunteer Force) As Delivered by Secretary of Defense Robert M. Gates, http://www.defense.gov/speeches/speech.aspx?speechid=1508 (Accessed November 2, 2011)

[26] Pew Research Center, "War and Sacrifice in the Post-9/11 Era The Military-Civilian Gap" http://www.pewsocialtrends.org/2011/10/05/war-and-sacrifice-in-the-post-911-era/ (Accessed November 2, 2011)

[27] Ibid.

[28] The Library of Congress, "H.R.2401--National Defense Authorization Act for Fiscal Year 1994 " http://thomas.loc.gov/cgi-bin/query/z?c103:H.R.2401.ENR: (Accessed 27 November, 2011)

[29] David Wood, "In the 10th Year of War, a Harder Army, a More Distant America", *Huffington Post*, September 9, 2010, http://www.politicsdaily.com/2010/09/09/in-the-10th-year-of-war-a-harder-army-a-more-distant-america/ (Accessed November 28, 2011)

[30] Lecture at Duke University (All Volunteer Force) As Delivered by Secretary of Defense Robert M. Gates, http://www.defense.gov/speeches/speech.aspx?speechid=1508 (Accessed November 2, 2011)

[31] Donna Mills, "Gap Between Military and Civilians Growing" Military.com News, November 28, 2011, http://www.military.com/news/article/2011/gap-between-military-and-civilians-growing.html#.Txo0SR7CdzY.email (Accessed December 2, 2011)

[32] Pew Research Center, "War and Sacrifice in the Post-9/11 Era The Military-Civilian Gap" http://www.pewsocialtrends.org/2011/10/05/war-and-sacrifice-in-the-post-911-era/ (Accessed November 2, 2011)

[33] David Wood, "Army's Generous Pay, Benefits: Are Skyrocketing Costs Sustainable?", Huffington Post, May 2, 2010, http://www.politicsdaily.com/2010/05/02/armys-generous-pay-benefits-are-skyrocketing-costs-sustainabl/ (Accessed March 19, 2012)

[34] Gregory Korte, "Fewer Members of Congress Today Also Served In Military" *USA TODAY* November 11, 2011, http://www.usatoday.com/news/washington/story/2011-11-10/congress-members-military-service/51159918/1 (Accessed November 25, 2011)

[35] Walter Oi, "The Virtue of an All Volunteer Force" The CATO Institute, July 29, 2003, http://www.cato.org/pub_display.php?pub_id=3182 (Accessed November 2, 2011)

[36] Lecture at Duke University (All Volunteer Force) As Delivered by Secretary of Defense Robert M. Gates, http://www.defense.gov/speeches/speech.aspx?speechid=1508 (Accessed November 2, 2011)

[37] David Alexander and Andrea Shalal-Esa, "Pentagon Plans to Cut Almost Half a Trillion Dollars in Military spending, cancel programs," *Reuters - National Post*, January 25, 2012 http://news.nationalpost.com/2012/01/25/pentagon-plans-to-cut-almost-half-a-trillion-dollars-in-military-spending-cancel-p/ (Accessed January 25, 2012)

[38] Steve Vogel, "White House Proposes Cuts in Military Recruiting Budget," *Washington Post*, May 11, 2009, http://www.washingtonpost.com/wpdyn/content/article/2009/05/10/AR2009051002172.html (Accessed March 19, 2012)

[39] Tim Kane, "Who Bears the Burden? Demographic Characteristics of U.S. Military Recruits Before and After 9/11," American Heritage Foundation, November 7, 2005, http://www.heritage.org/research/reports/2005/11/who-bears-the-burden-demographic-characteristics-of-us-military-recruits-before-and-after-9-11 (Accessed January 25, 2012)

[40] Lecture at Duke University (All Volunteer Force) As Delivered by Secretary of Defense Robert M. Gates, http://www.defense.gov/speeches/speech.aspx?speechid=1508 (Accessed November 2, 2011)

[41] GlobalSecurity.org, Base Realignment and Closure (BRAC) http://www.globalsecurity.org/military/facility/brac.htm (Accessed November 27, 2011)

[42] Lecture at Duke University (All Volunteer Force) As Delivered by Secretary of Defense Robert M. Gates, http://www.defense.gov/speeches/speech.aspx?speechid=1508 (Accessed November 2, 2011)

[43] Donna Mills, "Gap Between Military and Civilians Growing" Military.com News, http://www.military.com/news/article/2011/gap-between-military-and-civilians-growing.html#.Txo0SR7CdzY.email (Accessed December 2, 2011)

[44] Library of Congress, "War Powers Act", http://loc.gov/law/help/war-powers.php Library of Congress, (Accessed November 27, 2011)

[45] Yale Law School, "War Powers Resolution, Joint Resolution Concerning the War Powers of Congress and the President." Yale Law School, http://avalon.law.yale.edu/20th_century/warpower.asp (Accessed December 28, 2011)

[46] Library of Congress, "War Powers Act", http://loc.gov/law/help/war-powers.php, Library of Congress (Accessed November 27, 2011)

[47] Yale Law School, "War Powers Resolution, Joint Resolution Concerning the War Powers of Congress and the President," http://avalon.law.yale.edu/20th_century/warpower.asp (Accessed December 28, 2011)

[48] United Nations, Article 43, "Chapter VII: Action with Respect to Threats To the Peace, Breaches of the Peace, and Acts of Aggression," United Nations Charter, http://www.un.org/en/documents/charter/chapter7.shtml (Accessed March 19, 2012)

[49] Benjamin H. Friedman and Christopher Preble, "Refocusing U.S. Defense Strategy" CATO Institute, November 2010, http://www.downsizinggovernment.org/defense/refocusing_strategy (Accessed January 20, 2012)

[50] Office of Social Innovation and Civic Participation, "National and Community Service at CNCS", The White House, http://www.whitehouse.gov/administration/eop/sicp/initiatives/national-community-service, (Accessed February 29, 2012)

[51] Eleanor Golberg, "AmeriCorps, Eager To Expand, Backed By Presidential Candidates," *Huffington Post*, February 17, 2012, http://www.huffingtonpost.com/2012/02/17/americorps-presidential-candidates_n_1280100.html (Accessed February 29, 2012)

[52] Richard Dagger, "Republican Virtue, Liberal Freedom, and the Problem of Civic Service," Department of Political Science Arizona State University http://philosophy.la.psu.edu/jchristman/autonomy/Dagger.PDF, (Accessed February 29, 2012)

[53] Ibid.

[54] Ibid.

[55] Air Force Public Affairs, Defense Strategic Guidance, "Sustaining U.S. Global Leadership: Priorities for 21st Century Defense" Fact Sheet, 5 January 2012

[56] Lecture at Duke University (All Volunteer Force) As Delivered by Secretary of Defense Robert M. Gates, http://www.defense.gov/speeches/speech.aspx?speechid=1508 (Accessed November 2, 2011)

[57] Charlie Lewis, "A New Sparta: America's Threatening Civil-Military Gap," *Harvard Kennedy School Review* 2011 Edition, http://isites.harvard.edu/icb/icb.do?keyword=k74756&pageid =icb.page414666 (Accessed November 25, 2011)

[58] General Martin Dempsey, "Chairman's Strategic Direction to the Joint Force, 2012" Defense.gov, http://www.defense.gov/news/newsarticle.aspx?id=67077 (Accessed February 28, 2012)

www.ingramcontent.com/pod-product-compliance
Lightning Source LLC
Chambersburg PA
CBHW081810280526
45789CB00008B/3085